HurricaneOpal

Written by Robert R. O'Brien

Macmillan
McGraw-Hill

New York   Farmington

I woke up to the sound of sirens.

I was already sitting up in bed when my mom came in. "Okay, this is it, time to get out!" she said.

I pulled on my shoes. I had slept in my clothes. The moment we had dreaded had arrived. The sound of sirens mixed with another sound, a high, shrieking sound—the winds of Hurricane Opal.

We had seen the hurricane warning the night before. The news people said it was a class 5 storm, the most dangerous. We had just gone through a class 1 storm two months ago, and that was bad enough.

Mom told me to pack enough clothes for three days. I also packed some books, a deck of cards, and a canteen full of water.

Mom packed the car full of food, and took things that could never be replaced, like baby pictures.

"Why pack that stuff?" I asked. "We're just going to come back in a couple of days." I was wrong about that.

We got into the car. We had already put up storm shutters with the help of our neighbor, Mrs. Banning. There was nothing else to do but hope.

I noticed our neighbor's swing set. The wind was blowing the swing almost straight back. And the rain was going sideways.

A very strong gust of wind shook the car.

"Let's get out of here," said Mom.

We headed across the bridge. We live on an island. The bridge to it is about three miles long. We could see whitecaps on the bay. The bridge was full of cars.

It didn't take long for us to get stuck in traffic. Everybody was leaving at the same time! My mom got a worried look on her face. A trip that usually took 10 minutes took us an hour.

"That hurricane is moving faster than we are, I bet," my mom muttered. "We have to do something or we're going to be stuck."

I got the map out. My mom looked at it, then turned the car around. She found a different road and headed in another direction.

"This might not be the best way, but it's faster than the way we were going." My mom smiled at me. "We're not going to let a little hurricane scare us, are we?"

I smiled at her, but I was scared.

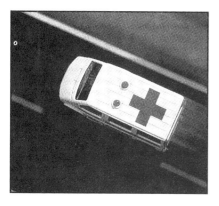

We started to really feel the wind. The rain was coming down so hard we could hardly see. The news announcer on the car radio said that the hurricane would hit soon.

We came up to a church and saw lots of cars in the parking lot. There was a Red Cross truck in the lot.

"That's a shelter," said my mom. "Let's go in."

There seemed to be hundreds of people inside. There was a desk where we had to sign in, and they showed us to our cots. There was a family with kids near my age next to us. I started playing cards with them, while my mom got some coffee and listened to the news on a portable TV.

They were saying that tornado warnings were up in many areas.

After a while, they gave soup and sandwiches to everybody. "Well, it's not home cooking, but it's good enough for me," I said to Mom. She laughed, but it didn't seem all that funny.

9

We had one bad scare later that night. The tornado warning siren went off, and we all had to move to the center of the shelter. Some folks cried, some folks prayed. My mom and I just hugged each other, and soon the "all clear" sounded. I wondered if it had been a false alarm.

We slept that night with about 500 neighbors. We didn't get much sleep. Some kids were crying, some grownups were snoring. But we were dry—and safe.

The next day we headed back home. It was sunny, with lots of white puffy clouds. Everything was wet. On the way back we saw trees blown down. We saw lots of police and National Guard trucks. We passed one house that had a big tree on the roof. Another place was torn apart by a tornado.

"Wow!" was all we could say.

When we got to the bridge we couldn't figure out why it looked different. Then we saw. There was seaweed hanging from parts of the bridge. The water had come up over the bridge! We could see a boat floating upside down as we crossed the bridge. We saw another boat up on the road as we got closer to our house.

"I don't like the looks of this," said my mom.

"Me neither," I replied.

We were stopped by police as we got near our street. "The damage is very bad in your area, folks. Be prepared for the worst, and be very careful."

We took the road leading to our street. Wood and stuff from people's houses was everywhere. Parking lots were still flooded, and places that had been lawns were now covered with sand. It looked like pictures I'd seen of blizzards, except it was all sand, not snow.

Finally we found our street, or what was left of it.
We later found out that huge waves had covered the
island. The waves pounded some of the houses flat.
Others were just gone.

We found ours. It was full of sand. Mrs. Banning's
refrigerator was in our living room. The waves had
knocked our front wall in. We both cried when we saw
it. I wanted to go in, but my mom wouldn't let me. We
tried to find our belongings, but all we found was the
top of our neighbor's swing, sticking out of the sand.

We went to another Red Cross shelter that night. We saw some of our neighbors and friends. There was lots of crying and hugging. But everybody was safe.

The next day we went to a special Red Cross office. People from all around the country had gathered there to help. A Red Cross volunteer gave my mom some papers that would help us get food and a place to stay. After we had a new place to live, the Red Cross would help us get the things we needed.

It was the first good feeling I'd had since we left our house.

We still have a long way to go before we are back to normal. We are living in an apartment until our house gets rebuilt. It's been hard to get over losing all our stuff. The apartment seems pretty empty, and I hate it when I go to look for something I know I used to have and then remember it's gone. But at least we are alive and well.

I just hope I never see another hurricane like Opal.